This book belongs to:

Published by Poggle Press, an imprint of
Indigo Timmins Ltd • Pure Offices • Leamington Spa • Warwickshire CV34 6WE

ISBN: 978-0-9573501-4-4

10 9 8 7 6 5 4 3 2 1

www.springboardstories.co.uk

Sports Day on Mount Olympus

Paul Mason

Illustrated by
Simon Walmesley & James Walmesley

A Poggle Press publication

For Mia and Milo

You can find some helpful hints on how to pronounce those tricky Greek names at the end of the book.

In days of old, in the time of legends, gods lived on Mount Olympus. High above the clouds, never rattled by winds or soaked by rain. Where the sun always shone from a clear blue sky.

It was sports day at Mount Olympus Primary School, and the stage was set for a truly Olympian contest....

The sand for the long-jump was raked silky and smooth, the hurdles were polished till they gleamed, the javelins fixed all straight and pointy.

On the field, the gods and goddesses of Mount Olympus practically crackled with excitement. They couldn't wait.

Sports day meant trophies! All glittery and golden. (And trophies look great on a bedroom shelf.)

Miss Hercules, teacher of 4B, cleared her voice.

'Aphrodite, Apollo, Ares, Artemis, Athena?'

'Present, Miss.'

'Demeter, Dionysus, Hephaestus, Hera, Hermes?'

'Good morning, Miss.'

'Poseidon and Zeus – stop that chatter, you two.'

'*Now where is Alexia?*' said Miss Hercules, looking around.

Little Alexia Alexopoulos was hidden in the crowd, her voice barely a whisper. '*Here, Miss Hercules.*'

'*Speak up my dear,*' said Miss Hercules, '*there's a good girl.*'

But Alexia found it hard to speak up. She was the only mortal at Mount Olympus. The only human. The only one who didn't have super powers.

No wonder she was as quiet as a goldfish with a sore throat.

Alexia wished her parents had never sent her to this school. But they had wanted the best primary in the land, and so here she was. The only normal kid in a school for gods.

It had been a hard year so far. Science fair, exams, talent show, all the same. Alexia Alexopoulos, bottom of the class.

What hope did she have of winning anything at sports day? No hope at all.

'*Right now, line up for the* sprints,' called Miss Hercules.

'*Watch this!*' said Hermes, the divine messenger, lacing up his winged sandals.

PAAAARP went the starting horn. Off went the class, thundering along the track like a stampede of shoppers on Christmas Eve. Hermes' feet barely touched the ground.

Alexia gave it everything she had. Her face was scorched red. But all the others were over the finish line long before her.

'*Well done, Hermes*,' said Alexia, panting and wheezing. '*Super running*.'

'*Not even puffed*,' said Hermes.

'*Archery contest*,' announced Miss Hercules.

'*My turn*,' said Artemis, goddess of the hunt, twirling her golden bow and making it sing like dad in the bathtub on a Friday night. Artemis drew three arrows, all at once. Then she let them fly.

1, 2, 3... bull's-eye!

All the other gods' arrows **zinged** into the targets too. Alexia **gritted** her teeth. She pulled back the string as far as she could. But her arrow misfired and hit the grass with a

thut!

'*Nice one, Artemis*,' said Alexia, rubbing her sore fingers. '*Super shooting.*'

'*Pipsqueak*,' said Artemis.

With every event, Alexia's face sunk lower and lower.

In the discus, Hephaestus, master blacksmith, threw his discus right over the fence and into the neighbour's bins. (He had to go and ask for it back.)

Alexia's flopped at her feet.

In the high-jump, bright-eyed Athena, goddess of wisdom, overshot the mat by miles and clattered onto the roof of the cafeteria, knocking plaster all over the sprouts. (Cook was not happy.)

Alexia whacked the bar off first go.

In the javelin, Zeus, lord of sky and thunder, launched his spear over the field and into the car park, scratching the headmaster's brand new sports chariot. (He got first place, and a detention at lunch time.)

Alexia's javelin barely got past her toes.

Alexia was playing fair. She was trying her hardest.

It was just hopeless.

At last it was time for the final contest of the competition. The cross-country.

The gods and goddesses strolled up to the starting line, sniggering and smiling like a troop of clowns with whoopee cushions. They'd all won a trophy or a ribbon. All but Alexia.

'*Pssst*,' whispered Dionysus, god of celebrations, to the others. '*I've hidden a hamper stuffed with snacks half-way round. How about we stop and have a picnic?*'

The other gods thought this was a great idea.
'*Why not?*' agreed Athena.

'*Sounds fun! After all, I could win this race in my sleep,*' thundered Zeus.

Alexia was appalled. '*But it's sports day. You're supposed to do your best.*'

The other gods just laughed. '*Suit yourself*, *Alexia*,' said Dionysus.

PAAARP went the horn and they were off – racing away into the distance. Alexia pumped her arms. She pumped her legs. She kept her eyes on the path. She decided she wouldn't worry about the others.

The gods and goddesses soon disappeared ahead of her, over the hill and far away. But when Alexia caught up to them she found them, true to their word, lounging on the grass next to the path.

Dionysus had opened up his picnic hamper and everyone was munching and having a good old time, laughing and playing games.

The gods all waved at Alexia as she ran past. They would run when they were good and ready.

'Why break a sweat *if you don't have to?'* said Artemis with her mouth full of crisps. (Prawn cocktail, her favourite.)

'*True*,' agreed Hephaestus, chomping on a sausage roll.

'No need to rush,' added Hermes who was lying sprawled on the grass. '*We'll overtake Alexia soon enough.*'

But Alexia kept her eyes on the path. She pumped her legs. She pumped her arms. She didn't worry about the others.

Up the grassy hill she ran, and down the other side. Over the stony bridge, and along the babbling stream.

Through the dark forest, and back out into the sunshine. Alexia just kept her eyes on the path.

And at last came a wonderful sight. The finish line. Alexia lifted her head and looked around. She could hardly believe it. There was no-one else to be seen. They were all too busy having fun.

Alexia used every last bit of strength she had. She ran for the ribbon, a smile spreading wide across her face.

Some time later the others came tearing down the path, pushing and shoving their way over the finish line.

'*I came first*,' announced Hermes.

'*Rubbish!*' roared Zeus. They began to squabble.

Miss Hercules was not impressed. She blasted her whistle.

'*None of you did. The* winner *is* Alexia,' she declared.
'*While you were being lazy and boastful,* Alexia just got on with it.'

The gods and goddesses looked down at their sandals, their faces red with embarrassment. Miss Hercules was right. They'd been too busy showing off, and they'd been caught.

Now they gathered around Alexia to congratulate her.

'Well done,' said Artemis.

'Epic!' agreed Athena with a smile.

'What an effort!' said Zeus.

'*I suppose you might even say it was a super human effort*,' smiled Miss Hercules.

Alexia beamed. Cross-country champion! She couldn't wait to tell Mum and Dad.

Need help with those Greek names?

Alexia – a-**lex**-ee-*uh*

Alexopoulous – a-lex-**op**-*uh*-lus

Aphrodite – af-r*oh*-**dy**-tee

Apollo – a-**pol**-*oh*

Ares – **air**-eez

Artemis – **ar**-ti-mis

Athena – a-**thee**-n*uh*

Demeter – di-**mee**-t*uh*

Dionysus – dy-*uh*-**ny**-sis

Hephaestus – h*eh*-**fes**-tus

Hera – **hee**-r*uh*

Hercules – **her**-kyoo-leez

Hermes – **her**-meez

Poseidon – p*uh*-**sy**-dun

Zeus – zee-**yoos**

(Of course, some people might say the names differently.)